LOVE AND THE TURNING YEAR
ONE HUNDRED MORE POEMS
FROM THE CHINESE

BOOKS BY KENNETH REXROTH

POEMS

The Collected Shorter Poems
The Collected Longer Poems
Sky Sea Birds Trees Earth House Beasts Flowers
New Poems
The Phoenix and the Tortoise

PLAYS

Beyond the Mountains

CRITICISM & ESSAYS

The Alternative Society
American Poetry in the Twentieth Century
Assays
Bird in the Bush
The Classics Revisited
Communalism, from the Neolithic to 1900
The Elastic Retort
With Eye and Ear

TRANSLATIONS

100 Poems from the Chinese
Love and the Turning Year: 100 More Chinese Poems
The Orchid Boat: The Women Poets of China
    (with Ling Chung)
100 French Poems
Poems from the Greek Anthology
100 Poems from the Japanese
100 More Japanese Poems *(forthcoming)*
30 Spanish Poems of Love and Exile
Selected Poems of Pierre Reverdy

AUTOBIOGRAPHY

An Autobiographical Novel

EDITOR

An Anthology of Pre-literate Poetry
The Continuum Poetry Series

LOVE AND THE TURNING YEAR
ONE HUNDRED MORE POEMS
FROM THE CHINESE

by

KENNETH REXROTH

A NEW DIRECTIONS BOOK

FOR CAROL

谷神不死是謂玄
牝玄牝之門是謂
天地根綿綿若存
用之不勤　泰雲書

TABLE OF CONTENTS

IX

x

XII

INTRODUCTION

This is a collection of translations from the Chinese done down the years solely to please myself. It is offered with no pretense to scholarship or to mastery of that complex subject, Sinology. I have translated the pieces I enjoyed reading and I have enjoyed translating them, so I hope readers will find them enjoyable.

We are often told that the Chinese seldom write love poems. This is not true. From the beginning in *The Book of Odes*, the *Shi Ching*, there is a great deal of Chinese love poetry. True, the Confucian scholar gentry were given to the amusing and ingenuous habit of interpreting these poems as political allegories, but they obviously are not. Even the English title of the collection is misleading. It should be *The Folk Song Classic*. Each dynasty has made collections of folk songs, most of them love songs, and the literary poets have written imitations of them. A large proportion of the poems in this book of mine are song poems and many of them are love poems.

Now that I have put them all together and read them over I realize that they need no explanatory introduction and only biographical notes. I have avoided poems with references to Chinese historical and literary figures or to Chinese customs and beliefs unknown in the West. I have tried to keep the transliteration of Chinese names simple and uniform, using the modified Wade system commonly used in America. This is not Chinese, of any period, but it will do. Vowels are pronounced as in Italian: *ai* is English "i", *ei* is "a", *ou* is "ow". *Ch' t', k', ts', p', tz'* may be pronounced as spelled, but rather sharply. Without apostrophe, *ch* is pronounced "dj"; *k* is pronounced "g"; *p* is pronounced "b"; *t* is pronounced "d"; *hs* is a palatalized "sh"; *j* is "r." *E* before "n" or *ng* is a mute "u." In *tse* or *tzu* the vowel scarcely exists. Lao Tzu, the Chinese philosopher, is pronounced something like "Lowds." The Chinese *Book of Changes, I Ching*, sometimes spelled "Yi King", is pronounced, using American spelling, "ee jing." The "Yi King" is a relic of the extremely misleading orthography invented by Max Müller for *The Sacred Books of the East*. German transliteration is much like the Wade. The French have several incongruous systems inconsistently used.

The literature of Chinese poetry in translation must have doubled in volume in the last fifteen years. The scholarship, the accuracy, and the understanding of Chinese critical values and literary references have vastly improved. As poetry, no recent translations can compare with those of Ezra Pound, Judith Gautier, Klabund, Witter Bynner or Amy Lowell, none of whom knew very much about the subject or understood the language. Most modern collections do have extensive introductions, notes and bibliography as well as clear explanations of the forms and esthetics of Chinese poetry. I hope this book will stimulate the reader to read everything he can get his hands on. My book is only a sample; it is limited to a few kinds of poetry, mostly poems of love, reverie, and meditation in the midst of nature. I do hope these are poems in their own right.

Like the *Three Hundred Poems of T'ang* and other Far Eastern anthologies, this "Hundred Poems" contains a few more for good measure and good luck.

K. R.

LOVE AND THE TURNING YEAR
ONE HUNDRED MORE POEMS
FROM THE CHINESE

A PRESENT FROM THE EMPEROR'S
NEW CONCUBINE

I took a piece of the rare cloth of Ch'i,
White silk glowing and pure as frost on snow,
And made you a fan of harmony and joy,
As flawlessly round as the full moon.
Carry it always, nestled in your sleeve.
Wave it and it will make a cooling breeze.
I hope, that when Autumn comes back
And the North wind drives away the heat,
You will not store it away amongst old gifts
And forget it, long before it is worn out.

LADY P'AN

AUTUMN WIND

The autumn wind blows white clouds
About the sky. Grass turns brown.
Leaves fall. Wild geese fly south.
The last flowers bloom, orchids
And chrysanthemums with their
Bitter perfume. I dream of
That beautiful face I can
Never forget. I go for
A trip on the river. The barge
Rides the current and dips with
The white capped waves. They play flutes
And drums, and the rowers sing.
I am happy for a moment
And then the old sorrow comes back.
I was young only a little while,
And now I am growing old.

THE EMPEROR WU OF HAN

FROM THE MOST DISTANT TIME

Majestic, from the most distant time,
The sun rises and sets.
Time passes and men cannot stop it.
The four seasons serve them,
But do not belong to them.
The years flow like water.
Everything passes away before my eyes.

THE EMPEROR WU OF HAN

IV

DRAFTED

They married us when they put
Up our hair. We were just twenty
And fifteen. And ever since,
Our love has never been troubled.
Tonight we have the old joy
In each other, although our
Happiness will soon be over.
I remember the long march
That lies ahead of me, and
Go out and look up at the stars,
To see how the night has worn on.
Betelgeuse and Antares
Have both gone out. It is time
For me to leave for far off
Battlefields. No way of knowing
If we will ever see each
Other again. We clutch each
Other and sob, our faces
Streaming with tears. Goodbye, dear.
Protect the Spring flowers of
Your beauty. Think of the days
When we were happy together.
If I live I will come back.
If I die, remember me always.

SU WU

DEW ON THE YOUNG GARLIC LEAVES

The dew on the garlic
Is gone soon after sunrise.
The dew that evaporated this morning
Will descend again in tomorrow's dawn.
Man dies and is gone,
And when has anybody ever come back?

T'IEN HUNG

VI

LIFE IS LONG

Bright green young grass comes up in the garden,
Wet with dew before the day gets warm.
The fecund Spring pours out its gifts.
All nature radiates a kind of glory.
A lonely girl thinks with dread
Of the coming Autumn, and the time
Of withering flowers and falling bright gold leaves.
The Great River flows steadily to the East.
When has anyone ever made it
Return to the Western Springs?
If, when you're young and fair,
You don't realize your possibilities,
When you get old you'll have nothing
But sorrow to look back on.

ANONYMOUS (HAN DYNASTY)

VII

HOME

At fifteen I joined the army.
At twenty-five I came home at last.
As I entered the village
I met an old man and asked him,
"Who lives in our house now?"
"Look down the street,
There is your old home."
Pines and cypresses grow like weeds.
Rabbits live in the dog's house.
Pigeons nest in the broken tiles.
Wild grass covers the courtyard.
Rambling vines cover the well.
I gather wild millet and make a pudding
And pick some mallows for soup.
When soup and pudding are done,
There is no one to share them.
I stand by the broken gate,
And wipe the tears from my eyes.

ANONYMOUS (HAN DYNASTY)

VIII

THIS MORNING OUR BOAT LEFT

This morning our boat left the
Orchid bank and went out through
The tall reeds. Tonight we will
Anchor under mulberries
And elms. You and me, all day
Together, gathering rushes.
Now it is evening, and see,
We have gathered just one stalk.

ANONYMOUS (SIX DYNASTIES)

IX

THE FISH WEEPS

The fish weeps in the
Dry riverbed. Too late he
Is sorry he flopped
Across the shallows. Now he
Wants to go back and
Warn all the other fishes.

ANONYMOUS (SIX DYNASTIES)

X

THE CUCKOO CALLS
FROM THE BAMBOO GROVE

The cuckoo calls from the bamboo grove.
Cherry blossoms litter the path.
A girl walks under the full moon,
Trailing her silk skirts in the grass.

ANONYMOUS (SIX DYNASTIES)

XI

IN SPRING WE GATHER
MULBERRY LEAVES

In Spring we gather mulberry leaves.
At the end of Summer we unwind the cocoons.
If a young girl works day and night,
How is she going to find time to get married.

ANONYMOUS (SIX DYNASTIES)

XII

NIGHT WITHOUT END

Night without end. I cannot sleep.
The full moon blazes overhead.
Far off in the night I hear someone call.
Hopelessly I answer, "Yes."

ANONYMOUS (SIX DYNASTIES)

XIII

WHAT IS THE MATTER WITH ME?

What is the matter with me?
With all the men in the world,
Why can I think only of you?

ANONYMOUS (SIX DYNASTIES)

XIV

BITTER COLD

Bitter cold. No one is abroad.
I have been looking everywhere for you.
If you don't believe me,
Look at my footprints in the snow.

ANONYMOUS (SIX DYNASTIES)

XV

I CAN NO LONGER UNTANGLE MY HAIR

I can no longer untangle my hair.
I feed on my own flesh in secret.
Do you want to measure how much I long for you?
Look at my belt, how loose it hangs.

ANONYMOUS (SIX DYNASTIES)

XVI

KILL THAT CROWING COCK

Kill that crowing cock.
Drive away the chattering birds.
Shoot the cawing crows.
I want this night to last
And morning never come back.
I don't want to see another dawn
For at least a year.

ANONYMOUS (SIX DYNASTIES)

XVII

THE GIRL BY GREEN RIVER

I stopped at her door for a drink of water.
It was a little house, just a few steps from the bridge.
She was a young girl,
And lived alone without a husband.

ANONYMOUS (SIX DYNASTIES)

XVIII

NIGHTFALL

Nightfall. He jumped over the hedge.
Daybreak. He opened the gate and went out.
He has taken his pleasure,
And thinks no more of me.

ANONYMOUS (SIX DYNASTIES)

XIX

MY LOVER WILL SOON BE HERE

My lover will soon be here.
He said he would come to the garden gate.
My mother is still up.
I can hear my heart beat
Like a sword on a shield.

ANONYMOUS (SIX DYNASTIES)

XX

OUR LITTLE SISTER IS WORRIED

Our little sister is worried.
How long should she wait
To get married?
She has often seen the wind
Blow the peach petals from the trees.
She has never seen it
Blow them back on the branches.

ANONYMOUS (SIX DYNASTIES)

XXI

THE MONTHS GO BY

The months go by like water in a waterfall.
Now the Autumn is fading away.
A cricket cries in the stillness.
And I am sad and lonely.

ANONYMOUS (SIX DYNASTIES)

XXII

ALL YEAR LONG

1

We break off a branch of poplar catkins.
A hundred birds sing in the tree.
Lying beneath it in the garden,
We talk to each other,
Our tongues in each other's mouth.

2

The sultry air is heavy with flower perfumes.
What is there better to do this hot night
Than throw off the covers
And lie together naked?

3

A cold wind blows open the window.
The moon looks in, full and bright.
Not a sound,
Not a voice,
In the night.
Then from behind the bed curtains,
Two giggles.

4

A freezing sky.
The year ends.
Icy winds whirl the snowflakes.
Under the covers
My darling is hotter than midsummer night.

ANONYMOUS (SIX DYNASTIES)

XXIII

DEEP NIGHT

Deep night. I cannot sleep.
I get up and sing softly to my lute.
Moonlight glows in the gauze curtains.
I open my night gown, and let
The fresh night air bathe my body.
A lonely wild goose cries out
In the distant meadow.
A night bird flies calling through the trees.
I come and go without rest.
What do I gain by it?
My mind is distracted by worries
That will never cease.
My heart is all bruised
By the troubled ghosts who haunt it.

YUAN CHI

XXIV

THUNDER

Thunder. My heart trembles.
I lift my head from my pillow and listen.
It is not a chariot.

FU HSUAN

XXV

SHE THINKS OF HER BELOVED

It is going to rain.
The fresh
Breeze rustles the leaves of the
Cinnamon tree. It scatters
The begonias on the earth.
The falling petals cannot
Be numbered. Scarlet leaves fly
In the wind. The wind raises
Whirls of dust. All the world trembles.
It blows over the gauze screen,
Chills my flesh
And disarranges
My hair. Desolate and alone
I dream of my beloved
At the edge of Heaven, far
Across towering mountain
Ranges and roaring rivers.
I watch the birds wheel in the
Starry sky. I wish they could
Carry a letter. But he
Is too far away, they would
Never find the way. Rivers
Flow to the sea. Nothing can
Make the current return to
Its source. Lustrous and perfumed,
The magnolias lose their petals
All through the day and the night
I loosen the agate pegs

Of the lute and put the jade
Flute back in its case. In the
Silence and solitude, the sound
Of my beating heart frightens me.
The moon breaks through the clouds. I try
To write a poem in the endless night.

LU CHI

VISIT TO THE MONASTERY
OF GOOD OMEN

I take horse before cockcrow
And arrive at the monastery
As the evening bell is ringing.
The smell of incense
Permeates the quiet air.
The new moon sets over the edge of the forest.
The home of the men of peace and order
Has been loaned to me
As refuge until day dawns.
No one will follow me tonight
Along the road through the deep fir forest.
Only the chanting of the monks
Echoes between the darkening trees.

LU CHI

XXVII

IN MOURNING FOR HIS DEAD WIFE

Winter and Spring have come and gone.
Once more Autumn overtakes
Summer. She has returned to
The Hidden Springs. And all the
World separates us forever.
Who will listen to my secrets
Now? Who will I live for now?
I try to do my job at Court,
And reluctantly go through
The motions of duty, and
Take up the tasks I had dropped.
When I come home I can think
Only of her. When I come
In our room I expect to see her.
I catch her shadow on the
Screens and curtains. Her letters
Are the most precious examples
Of calligraphy. Her perfume
Still haunts the bedroom. Her clothes
Still hang there in the closet.
She is always alive in
My dreams. I wake with a start.
She vanishes. And I
Am overwhelmed with sorrow.
Two birds made a nest and then
There was only one. A pair
Of fishes were separated
And lost in the current.

The Autumn wind blows. The morning
Is misty, with dripping eaves.
All through the troubled night I was
Not able to forget in sleep.
I hope the time will come when
I am calm enough to beat
On a pot like Chuang Tsu did
In mourning for his dead wife.

P'AN YUEH (P'AN YENG JEN)

XXVIII

I RETURN TO THE PLACE I WAS BORN

From my youth up I never liked the city.
I never forgot the mountains where I was born.
The world caught me and harnessed me
And drove me through dust, thirty years away from home.
Migratory birds return to the same tree.
Fish find their way back to the pools where they were
                                                    hatched.
I have been over the whole country,
And have come back at last to the garden of my
                                                    childhood.
My farm is only ten acres.
The farm house has eight or nine rooms.
Elms and willows shade the back garden.
Peach trees stand by the front door.
The village is out of sight.
You can hear dogs bark in the alleys,
And cocks crow in the mulberry trees.
When you come through the gate into the court
You will find no dust or mess.
Peace and quiet live in every room.
I am content to stay here the rest of my life.
At last I have found myself.

T'AO YUAN MING (TAO CHIN)

XXIX

BY T'ING YANG WATERFALL

A strange, beautiful girl
Bathes her white feet in the flowing water.
The white moon, in the midst of the clouds,
Is far away, beyond the reach of man.

HSIEH LING YUEN

XXX

VIATICUM

When you go ten miles away
I'll go along for nine miles.
Then I'll leave you a hairpin
As a compass for your route.

PAO YU

XXXI

FAREWELL TO FAN YUN AT AN CH'ENG

Back in our young days whenever
We had to part we expected
To meet again. Today we
Are old and worn and we haven't
So many goodbyes left us.
Don't say, "Just one cup of wine."
How do you know when you'll get a chance
To drink another stirrup cup?
You say, "At least we can meet in dreams."
How do you know we will happen
On the way to each other
In our sleep? If we don't, it
Won't be much consolation.

SHEN YUEH

XXXII

FAREWELL TO SHEN YUEH

Heading East or West, down the
Many years, how often we
Have separated here at
Lo Yang Gate. Once when I left
The snow flakes seemed like flower
Petals. Now today the petals
Seem like snow.

FAN YUN

XXXIII

FREEZING NIGHT

The night is full of storm clouds.
Overhead the wild geese are frightened,
And cry out with anxiety in the murky darkness.
The icy hills are covered with dense fog.
The only thing visible
Is a beautiful shadow on a gleaming gauze window
                                        curtain.
Above the clouds the white moon is cold.
Under the clouds the storm wind is cold.
Heart full of sorrow,
Tears dried up with sorrow,
The unbearable sorrow,
Of a heart filled with love –
How can I go on under the beating storm of my thoughts?

T'AO HUNG CHING (T'AO T'UNG MING)

XXXIV

THE MORNING SUN SHINES

The morning sun shines
Through the filigree shutters.
A wind full of light
Blows open her thin gauze robe.
A sly smile comes on her lips.
Her moth eyebrows arch
Over her beautiful eyes.

THE EMPEROR WU OF LIANG

XXXV

WATER LILIES BLOOM

Water lilies bloom on the Great River.
Brilliant red on the green water.
Their color is the same as our hearts.
Their roots branch off.
Ours cannot be separated.

THE EMPEROR WU OF LIANG

XXXVI

THE TRAVELER

The traveler with his heavy heart
Goes off alone for a thousand miles,
On the dark river in the pouring rain,
White caps scudding before the wind.

HO HSUN

XXXVII

SPRING BREEZE

You can't see it or hear it,
It is so soft. But it is strong enough
To dust the mirror with pollen,
And thrum the strings of the lute.

HO HSUN

XXXVIII

FLYING PETALS

The new peach blossoms are glowing.
They fill the world with perfume.
Swallows fly through drifting petals.
The young leaves have a bitter smell.
Flying petals settle in the dew basins.
We arrange the branches in vases
And fill the house with beauty.
The petals sprinkle the old willow by the window
With vivid pink and white
Like rouge and powder.

EMPEROR CH'IEN WEN OF LIANG
(HSIAO KANG)

XXXIX

RISING IN WINTER

The winter morning sunrise
Shines on the rafters.
In spite of herself she gets
Out of bed. She wraps herself
In her bamboo dressing gown.
She polishes her mirror.
At this hour nobody
Is watching. What good does it
Do to paint her face so early?

EMPEROR CH'IEN WEN OF LIANG
(HSIAO KANG)

XL

THE NEW WIFE

Day after day my silk dresses grow more loose.
The peach and plum blossoms are fading.
I dream of my young husband who never comes home.
When he does he will no longer recognize me.

NG SHAO

XLI

SPRING RIVER FLOWERS MOON NIGHT

The river is smooth and calm this evening.
The Spring flowers bloom.
The moon floats on the current.
The tide carries the stars.

THE EMPEROR YANG OF SUI

XLII

HOMECOMING

I was a boy when I left home.
I come back an old man.
I think I remember the country dialect,
But my hair has turned white since I spoke it.
Children stare at me.
Nobody understands me.
They look at me and laugh, and say,
"Where do you come from, Milord?"

HO CH'E CH'ANG

XLIII

SINCE YOU LEFT

Since you left, my lover,
I can't take care of myself.
I do nothing but think of you.
I fade like the waning moon.

CH'ANG CH'U LING

NIGHT ON THE GREAT RIVER

We anchor the boat alongside a hazy island.
As the sun sets I am overwhelmed with nostalgia.
The plain stretches away without limit.
The sky is just above the tree tops.
The river flows quietly by.
The moon comes down amongst men.

MENG HAO JAN

RETURNING BY NIGHT TO LU-MEN

I can hear the evening bell
In the mountain temple ringing
Above the voices of people
Calling for the ferry at
Fisherman's Crossing, and others
Going home to the village
Along the river beaches.
I take the boat back to Lu-Men.
On the mountain the moon shines
Through misty trees. At last I find
The ancient cabin of Lord P'ang,
Hidden by the cliffs,
On a path through the pines,
Where all is eternal peace,
And only a solitary
Man comes and goes by himself.

MENG HAO JAN

XLVI

A MOUNTAIN SPRING

There is a brook in the mountains,
Nobody I ask knows its name.
It shines on the earth like a piece
Of the sky. It falls away
In waterfalls, with a sound
Like rain. It twists between rocks
And makes deep pools. It divides
Into islands. It flows through
Calm reaches. It goes its way
With no one to mind it. The years
Go by, its clear depths never change.

CH'U CH'UANG I

XLVII

EVENING IN THE GARDEN
CLEAR AFTER RAIN

Fifth month, golden plums are ripe;
The horizon is hazy; the evening dewfall heavy;
The grass along the lane is bright green.
The sun sets in burning clouds.
The old gardener is glad the rains are over.
He puts the damp mats out to dry
And sets to work repairing the collapsed mud walls.
Twilight, the sky is crystal clear.
The children dance with joy.
They shout and splash in the puddles.
All the world has been made new.
I walk in the garden without a coat.
The hedges are still wet and glittering.
The pond shimmers with a thousand rippling images.
They no sooner appear than
They are erased and appear again.
The beautiful trees are like my heart,
Swelling with boundless happiness.

CH'U CH'UANG I

XLVIII

COUNTRY HOUSE

I planted a hundred mulberry trees
And thirty acres of rice.
Now I have plenty of silk and grain,
And can afford to entertain my friends.
In the Spring I plant rice.
In the Autumn I gather chrysanthemums
And perfume the wine with their petals.
My wife enjoys being hospitable.
My children like to help serve.
Late afternoon, we give a picnic
At the back of the overgrown garden
In the shade of the elms and willows.
My friends drink until they are inspired.
The fresh breezes cool the heat of the day.
After everyone has gone home,
I walk out under the Milky Way,
And look up at the countless stars
That watch me from heaven.
I still have plenty of jugs in the cellar.
Nobody will prevent me
From opening some more tomorrow.

CH'U CH'UANG I

XLIX

TEA

By noon the heat became unbearable.
The birds stopped flying
And went to roost exhausted.
Sit here in the shade of the big tree.
Take off your hot woolen jacket.
The few small clouds floating overhead
Do nothing to cool the heat of the sun.
I'll put some tea on to boil
And cook some vegetables.
It's a good thing you don't live far.
You can stroll home after sunset.

CH'U CH'UANG I

AUTUMN TWILIGHT IN THE MOUNTAINS

In the empty mountains after the new rain
The evening is cool. Soon it will be Autumn.
The bright moon shines between the pines.
The crystal stream flows over the pebbles.
Girls coming home from washing in the river
Rustle through the bamboo grove.
Lotus leaves dance behind the fisherman's boat.
The perfumes of Spring have vanished
But my guests will long remember them.

WANG WEI

AUTUMN

It has turned cold.
The mountains grow more vast and more blue.
The Autumn waterfalls are louder.
I take my cane and go out the gate for a walk.
I can hear the last crickets
Singing in the chilly evening.
I am happy. The rays of the setting sun
Shine through the evening smoke
That hovers over the village.
I throw back my head,
Drunk with beauty,
And sing the "Willow Song"
At the top of my lungs.

WANG WEI

LII

TWILIGHT COMES

Twilight comes over the monastery garden.
Outside the window the trees grow dim in the dusk.
Woodcutters sing coming home across the fields.
The chant of the monks answers from the forest.
Birds come to the dew basins hidden amongst the flowers.
Off through the bamboos someone is playing a flute.
I am still not an old man,
But my heart is set on the life of a hermit.

WANG WEI

LIII

DEEP IN THE MOUNTAIN WILDERNESS

Deep in the mountain wilderness
Where nobody ever comes
Only once in a great while
Something like the sound of a far off voice,
The low rays of the sun
Slip through the dark forest,
And gleam again on the shadowy moss.

WANG WEI

BIRD AND WATERFALL MUSIC

Men sleep. The cassia blossoms fall.
The Spring night is still in the empty mountains.
When the full moon rises,
It troubles the wild birds.
From time to time you can hear them
Above the sound of the flooding waterfalls.

WANG WEI

LV

SPRING SORROW

Drive off that golden oriole.
Don't let him sing on the branch
By my window. His song called me
Back from a far off desert fort.

CH'IN CH'ANG SIU

A SORROW IN THE HAREM

Withered flowers fill the courtyard.
Moss creeps into the great hall.
On both sides everything was said long ago.
The smell of perfume still lingers in the air.

WANG CHANG LING

LVII

SPRING RAIN

A good rain knows its season.
It comes at the edge of Spring.
It steals through the night on the breeze
Noiselessly wetting everything.
Dark night, the clouds black as the roads,
Only a light on a boat gleaming.
In the morning, thoroughly soaked with water,
The flowers hang their heavy heads.

TU FU

LVIII

BY THE CITY GATE

A year ago today by
This very gate your face and
The peach blossoms mirrored each
Other. I do not know where
Your beautiful face has gone.
There are only peach blossoms
Flying in the Spring wind.

TS'UI HAO

NIGHT AT ANCHOR BY MAPLE BRIDGE

The moon sets. A crow caws.
Frost fills the sky.
Maple leaves fall on the river.
The fishermen's fires keep me awake.
From beyond Su Chou
The midnight bell on Cold Mountain
Reaches as far as my little boat.

CHANG CHI

THE BIRDS FROM THE MOUNTAINS

Their feathers were like white silk.
They roosted every night in
The tree by our house. Tonight
A monkey came to pick the
Chestnuts, and two by two they
Flew away towards the moon.

CHANG CHI

LXI

MOUNT T'AI P'ING

Steep cliffs pierce the sky.
Dense forest hides the sun.
Spring never comes in the dark canyons.
Snow lasts all Summer on the frozen summits.

CH'IEN CH'I

LXII

VISIT TO THE HERMIT TS'UI

Moss covered paths between scarlet peonies,
Pale jade mountains fill your rustic windows.
I envy you, drunk with flowers,
Butterflies swirling in your dreams.

CH'IEN CH'I

LXIII

SNOW ON LOTUS MOUNTAIN

Sunset. Blue peaks vanish in dusk.
Under the Winter stars
My lonely cabin is covered with snow.
I can hear the dogs barking
At the rustic gate.
Through snow and wind
Someone is coming home.

LIU CH'ANG CH'ING

AMONGST THE CLIFFS

The path up the mountain is hard
To follow through the tumbled rocks.
When I reach the monastery
The bats are already flying.
I go to the guest room and sit
On the steps. The rain is over.
The banana leaves are broad.
The gardenias are in bloom.
The old guest master tells me
There are ancient paintings on the
Walls. He goes and gets a light.
I see they are incomparably
Beautiful. He spreads my bed
And sweeps the mat. He serves me
Soup and rice. It is simple
Food but nourishing. The night
Goes on as I lie and listen
To the great peace. Insects chirp
And click in the stillness. The
Pure moon rises over the ridge
And shines in my door. At daybreak
I get up alone. I saddle
My horse myself and go my way.
The trails are all washed out.
I go up and down, picking my
Way through storm clouds on the mountain.
Red cliffs, green waterfalls, all
Sparkle in the morning light.

I pass pines and oaks ten men
Could not reach around. I cross
Flooded streams. My bare feet stumble
On the cobbles. The water roars.
My clothes whip in the wind. This
Is the only life where a man
Can find happiness. Why do I
Spend my days bridled like a horse
With a cruel bit in his mouth?
If I only had a few friends
Who agreed with me we'd retire
To the mountains and stay till our lives end.

HAN YU

LXV

DRINKING WITH FRIENDS AMONGST
THE BLOOMING PEONIES

We had a drinking party
To admire the peonies.
I drank cup after cup till
I was drunk. Then to my shame
I heard the flowers whisper,
"What are we doing, blooming
For these old alcoholics?"

LIU YU HSI

71

LXVI

TO THE TUNE "GLITTERING SWORD HILTS"

I have always been sorry
Our words were so trivial
And never matched the depths
Of our thoughts. This morning
Our eyes met,
And a hundred emotions
Rushed through our veins.

LIU YU HSI

LXVII

THE BAMBOO BY LI CH'E YUN'S WINDOW

Don't cut it to make a flute.
Don't trim it for a fishing
Pole. When the grass and flowers
Are all gone, it will be beautiful
Under the falling snow flakes.

PO CHU I

LXVIII

VIEW FROM THE CLIFFS

I climb the cold mountain by
A steep path through the rocks,
To my little cabin in
The place where the clouds are born.
I halt my cart and look out
Over the forest of maples
In the sunset. The frosted
Leaves are more brilliant than
Any flowers of Spring.

TU MU

74

LXIX

WE DRINK FAREWELL

Chilled by excess of passion,
Unsmiling, we drink farewell.
The candle, overcome by sorrow,
Weeps for us all through the night.

TU MU

LXX

I WAKE UP ALONE

Gentle breeze, morning dew,
Behind my bed curtains,
I wake up alone.
Orioles sing. Flowers bloom.
Who cares if Spring has come?

LI SHANG YIN

LXXI

WHEN WILL I BE HOME?

When will I be home? I don't know.
In the mountains, in the rainy night,
The Autumn lake is flooded.
Someday we will be back together again.
We will sit in the candlelight by the West window,
And I will tell you how I remembered you
Tonight on the stormy mountain.

LI SHANG YIN

LXXII

EVENING COMES

Evening comes. My mind is troubled.
I go for a drive past the tombs on the ancient plain.
The beauty of the sunset is heart rending.
The shadows of night come like remembered sorrow.

LI SHANG YIN

LXXIII

HER BEAUTY IS HIDDEN

Her beauty is hidden by a cloudy screen.
The imperial city is drowned in the Spring night.
She foolishly married an important bureaucrat.
He prefers the dawn audience to her scented bed.

LI SHANG YIN

LXXIV

THE CANDLE CASTS DARK SHADOWS

The candle casts dark shadows
On the mother of pearl screen.
Slowly, slowly, the Milky Way
Goes down the sky. The stars go out.
Girl in the moon, are you sorry
You stole the herb of immortality,
And night after night have to
Watch over the distant, emerald
Sea and the boundless jeweled sky?

LI SHANG YIN

LXXV

THE OLD HAREM

The old harem is quiet and deserted.
The flowers still bloom in the neglected courtyard.
A few white haired old women sit in the sun,
Idly gossiping of the days of the dead emperor.

LI SHANG YIN

LXXVI

A FAITHFUL WIFE

You know I have a husband.
Why did you give me these two glowing pearls?
I could acknowledge your love
And sew them on my red dress,
But I come from a noble family,
Courtiers of the Emperor.
My husband is an officer in the Palace Guard.
Of course I realize that your intentions
Are pure as the light of Heaven,
But I have sworn to be true to my husband
In life and in death.
So I must give back your beautiful pearls,
With two tears to match them.
Why didn't I meet you
Before I was married?

CHANG CHI

LXXVII

THE RUSTIC TEMPLE IS HIDDEN

The rustic temple is hidden
Amongst the trees. The mists of
Evening drift round the mountain
Cabin. Spring grows old. No one
Comes by. Undisturbed the gold
Dust of pine pollen covers the path.

CHU CHEN PO

LXXVIII

HEDGEHOG

He ambles along like a walking pin cushion,
Stops and curls up like a chestnut burr.
He's not worried because he's so little.
Nobody is going to slap him around.

CHU CHEN PO

LXXIX

TO AN OLD TUNE

Men hope to last a hundred years.
Flowers last just for a Spring.
Just one day of wind and rain,
And they are scattered on the earth.
If they knew what was happening to them,
They would be as miserable as men.

LU KUEI MENG

IN THE MOUNTAINS AS AUTUMN BEGINS

Cold air drains down from the peaks.
Frost lies all around my cabin.
The trees are bare. Weak sunlight
Shines in my window. The pond
Is full and still. The water
Is motionless. I watch the
Gibbons gather fallen fruit.
All night I hear the deer stamping
In the dry leaves. My old harp
Soothes all my trouble away.
The clear voice of the waterfall
In the night accompanies my playing.

WEN T'ING YEN

LXXXI

PASSING A RUINED PALACE

Heavy dew. Thick mist. Dense grass.
Trees grow on the broken balconies.
Willows choke the empty moat.
Fallen flowers litter the courts.
The drunken parties are long gone.
At the fifth watch, under the waning moon,
A nightingale is singing.
I dream of those perfumed lives
That died in inconsolable grief.
The ancient palace is a heap of ruins.
The road has vanished.
The landscape is the same.
The works of men are being obliterated.
When I pass by the broken gate
My horse whinnies again and again.

WEN T'ING YEN

LXXXII

CROSSING HAN RIVER

Beyond the mountain passes
There were no more letters.
Winter is gone, now it is Spring.
As I near home
I am filled with worry.
I am afraid to question
The travelers who come along the road.

LI P'IN

LXXXIII

REMEMBERING MIN CH'E
A LETTER TO HIS BROTHER SU CHE

What is our life on earth?
A flock of migrating geese
Rest for a moment on the snow,
Leave the print of their claws
And fly away, some East, some West.
The old monk is no more.
There is a new gravestone for him.
On the broken wall of his hut
You can't find the poems we wrote.
There's nothing to show we've ever been there.
The road was long. We were tired out.
My limping mule brayed all the way.

SU TUNG P'O

CLEAR BRIGHT

On the slopes of the mountain
From North to South
The fields are covered with tombs.
On the Feast of Clear Bright
They make sacrifices at every grave.
Bloody tears, sobs like horns,
Voices like screech owls.
After sunset the foxes come back
To their beds under the mounds,
And men and girls come,
And on top of the graves,
Make love by lantern light.
My friend, while you're alive
And have wine, use it to get drunk.
There'll be no second helpings
When you get to the Nine Springs.

HUANG T'ING CH'IEN

A WEARY SONG TO A SLOW SAD TUNE

Search. Search. Seek. Seek.
Cold. Cold. Clear. Clear.
Sorrow. Sorrow. Pain. Pain.
Hot flashes. Sudden chills.
Stabbing pains. Slow agonies.
I drink two cups, then three bowls,
Of clear wine until I can't
Stand up against a gust of wind.
Wild geese fly over head.
They wrench my heart.
They were our friends in the old days.
Gold chrysanthemums litter
The ground, pile up, faded, dead.
This season I could not bear
To pick them. All alone,
Motionless at my window,
I watch the gathering shadows.
Fine rain sifts through the *wu t'ung* trees,
And drips, drop by drop, through the dusk.
What can I ever do now?
How can I drive off this word –
Hopelessness?

THE POETESS LI CH'ING CHAO

LXXXVI

TO THE TUNE "THE BOAT OF STARS"

Year after year I have watched
My jade mirror. Now my rouge
And creams sicken me. One more
Year that he has not come back.
My flesh shakes when a letter
Comes from South of the River.
I cannot drink wine since he left,
But the Autumn has drunk up all my tears.
I have lost my mind, far off
In the jungle mists of the South.
The gates of Heaven are nearer
Than the body of my beloved.

THE POETESS LI CH'ING CHAO

LXXXVII

TO THE TUNE
"DRUNK UNDER FLOWER SHADOWS"

Light mist, then dense fog –
A day endless as my sorrow.
Rare incense smoke curls from the
Mouth of the gold animal.
Once more it is the Ninth Day
Of the Ninth Month. I lie restless
On my brocade pillow, under
The gauze curtains, until, past
Midnight, a chill seeps into me.
In the East Enclosed Garden
We got drunk one evening.
The wine's secret perfume has never
Left my sleeves. No one else notices,
But it carries my soul away.
Now when the West wind flaps the screens,
I am more frail than the orchid petals.

THE POETESS LI CH'ING CHAO

TO THE TUNE "SPRING AT WU LING"

The gentle breeze has died down.
The perfumed dust has settled.
It is the end of the time
Of flowers. Evening falls
And all day I have been too
Lazy to comb my hair.
The toilet articles are there,
But the man is gone away.
All effort would be wasted.
When I try to sing, my tears
Choke me. I dreamed my flower boat
Carried me to him, but I
Know so fragile a vessel
Won't bear such a weight of sorrow.

THE POETESS LI CH'ING CHAO

LXXXIX

TO THE TUNE
"CUTTING A FLOWERING PLUM BRANCH"

Red lotus incense fades on
The jewelled curtain. Autumn
Comes again. Gently I open
My silk dress and float alone
On the orchid boat. Who can
Take a letter beyond the clouds?
Only the wild geese come back
And write their ideograms
On the sky under the full
Moon that floods the West Chamber.
Flowers, after their kind, flutter
And scatter. Water after
Its nature, when spilt, at last
Gathers again in one place.
Creatures of the same species
Long for each other. But we
Are far apart and I have
Grown learned in sorrow.
Nothing can make it dissolve
And go away. One moment,
It is on my eyebrows.
The next, it weighs on my heart.

THE POETESS LI CH'ING CHAO

95

TO THE TUNE "A LONELY FLUTE
ON THE PHOENIX TERRACE"

I let the incense grow cold
In the burner. My brocade
Bed covers are tumbled as
The waves of the sea. Idle
Since I got up, I neglect
My hair. My toilet table
Is unopened. I leave the
Curtains down until the sun shines
Over the curtain rings.
This separation prostrates me.
The distance terrifies me.
I long to talk to him once more.
Down the years there will be only
Silence between us forever now.
I am emaciated, but
Not with sickness, not with wine,
Not with Autumn.
It is all over now forever.
I sing over and over
The song, "Goodbye Forever."
I keep forgetting the words.
My mind is far off in Wu Ling.
My body is a prisoner
In this room above the misty
River, the jade green river,
That is the only companion
Of my endless days. I stare

Down the river, far off, into
The distance. I stare far away.
My eyes find only my own sorrow.

THE POETESS LI CH'ING CHAO

XCI

SPRING MORNING

Dawn. Birds sing in the courtyard.
Spring overwhelms the forest
With flowers. All of a sudden
A beautiful poem appears
Before me. When I try to catch
It in the nets of prosody
I can't find them.

CH'EN YU YI

ENLIGHTENMENT

A breach of clear heaven opens
In the clouds. To the Southwest
The River stretches smooth and still.
There are tattered skirts of mist
On the sandbars. On the wall a
Magpie shakes his wet feathers
And scolds. Beyond the rooftops
The thunder is still grumbling.
I decide to profit by
The fresh air and pay myself
A small sum of peace. I hunt
Busily for some fine words
To announce the return of
Good weather, and the splendor
Of the evening, but I have
No one to share them with.
So I sit quietly and watch
The Milky Way light up.
I am suffused with its glow.
All my spirit is illuminated.

CH'EN YU YI

99

XCIII

RAIN ON THE RIVER

We cross the river over dark waves
Through dense fog and tie up the little boat
Under the bank to a willow.
I wake up heavy with wine in the middle of the night.
The lamp is only a
Smoky red coal. I lie listening to the
Hsiao hsiao of the rain on the bamboo roof
Of the cabin.

LU YU

XCIV

IN THE COUNTRY

My neighbor runs to me with
The news, "Look out your window!"
For days the mountain was
Invisible. This morning
It shines bright and new
As though it had been washed.

LU YU

LAZY

Once we had a knocker
On the gate.
Now we seldom
Open it. I don't want people
Scuffing up the green moss.
The sun grows warm. Spring has really
Come at last. Sometimes you
Can hear faintly on the gentle
Breeze the noise of the street.
My wife is reading the classics.
She asks me the meaning
Of ancient characters.
My son begs for a sip of wine.
He drinks the whole cup before
I can stop him.
Is there anything
Better than an enclosed garden
With yellow plums and purple plums
Planted alternately?

LU YU

INSOMNIA

Even when I fall asleep early,
My nights are long and full of bitterness.
Tonight, tortured with insomnia,
Memories of the past flood back
Until they have exhausted me.
Alone in the house beside a smoky lamp,
I rub my heavy eyelids
And idly turn the pages of my notebook.
Again and again I scratch my head
And trim my brush and stir the heavy ink.
The hours go by. The moon comes
And stands in the open door,
White and shining like molten silver.
Suddenly I am back, sailing on Ts'ai Fong River
With the fellows of my youth,
Back in Yuen village.
Oh wonderful mountains! Oh noble boys!
How is it that I have lived so long
And never once gone back to visit you?

LU YU

XCVII

TO AN OLD TUNE

In my young days I never
Tasted sorrow. I wanted
To become a famous poet.
I wanted to get ahead
So I pretended to be sad.
Now I am old and have known
The depths of every sorrow,
And I am content to loaf
And enjoy the clear Autumn.

HSIN CH'I CHI

XCVIII

HER HUSBAND ASKS HER TO BUY
A BOLT OF SILK

The wind is cruel. Her clothes are worn and thin.
The weaver girl blows on her fingers.
Beside the dark window, back and forth,
She throws a shuttle like a lump of ice.
During the short Winter day
She can scarcely weave one foot of brocade.
And you expect me to make a folk song of this,
For your silken girls to sing?

THE POETESS CH'EN T'AO

XCIX

SEVENTH DAY SEVENTH MONTH

We lie one against the other,
Tangle together like painted
Clouds on a screen, then,
Thighs enlaced, heads together
On the pillow we sing softly
To the full moon and watch time pass.
The declining moon marks the hours.
Suddenly we are seized by grief and fear.
Three o'clock in the morning
Has gone by but we cannot
Get enough of one another. Insatiable
Passion, night swift as the shuttle
In the loom. Oh Heaven, what is
Your price for one more hour?

KUAN YUN SHE

C

SORROW

The white moon gleams through scudding
Clouds in the cold sky of the Ninth
Month. The white frost weighs down the
Leaves and the branches bend low
Over the freezing water.
All alone I sit by my
Window. The crushing burden
Of the passing days never
Grows lighter for an instant.
I write poems, change and correct them,
And finally throw them away.
Gold crysanthemums wither
Along the balcony. Hard
Cries of migrating storks fall
Heavily from the icy sky.
All alone by my window
Hidden in my empty room,
All alone, I burn incense,
And dream in the smoke, all alone.

THE POETESS CHU SHU CHEN

CI

LOST

Last year at the Feast of Lanterns,
The flower stalls were bright as day.
When the moon rose over the willows,
I walked in the moonlight with my beloved.
Another year – the same holiday –
The moon and the lanterns have not changed.
My lover is lost, I cannot find him,
And I wipe away my tears with my sleeve.

THE POETESS CHU SHU CHEN

TO THE TUNE "THE FAIR MAID OF YU"

Once when young I lay and listened
To the rain falling on the roof
Of a brothel. The candle light
Gleamed on silk and silky flesh.
Later I heard it on the
Cabin roof of a small boat
On the Great River, under
Low clouds, where wild geese cried out
On the Autumn storm. Now I
Hear it again on the monastery
Roof. My hair has turned white.
Joy – sorrow – parting – meeting –
Are all as though they had
Never been. Only the rain
Is the same, falling in streams
On the tiles, all through the night.

CHIANG CHIEH

CIII

WIND TOSSED DRAGONS

The shadows of the cypresses
On the moonlit avenue
To the abandoned palace
Weave in tangles on the road
Like great kelp in the depths of the sea.
When the palace was full of people
I used to see this all the time
And never noticed how beautiful it was.
Mid-Autumn full moon, the luminous night
Is like a boundless ocean. A wild
Wind blows down the empty birds' nests
And makes a sound like the waves of the sea
In the branches of the lonely trees.

HSIEH NGAO

CIV

THE OLD COWBOY

Other oxen have long curly horns.
My ox has a long bare tail.
I tag along behind,
Holding it like a flute or a whip.
We wander from the Southern hill
To the Eastern cliffs.
When he is tired or hungry,
I always know what to do.
Sunset, my ox ambles slowly home.
As he walks along,
I sing a song.
When he lies down,
I do too.
At night in the barn
I sleep by his side.
I am old. I take care of my ox.
I have nothing else to do.
I only worry that some day
They will sell my ox
To pay their taxes.

KAO CHI

AT YUEN YANG·LAKE

Green and blue the reedy shallows
Of Yuen Yang Lake stretch away
To the horizon. Boating in
The beautiful Spring weather,
A sudden shower drives me
To the shelter of a tree
Overhanging the bank.
Rising mist envelops the
Flowering peach trees. Rain and fog
Obscure everything. I
Can no longer tell where I am.
I try to find my way back.
At last I see the willows
Beside my landing and boat house.
Birds are singing in the trees.
When I come ashore I discover
I have been gone for ten years.

WU WEI YE

CVI

AT CH'EN CH'U

The river is lined with the
Huts of the fishermen. Floating
Poplar leaves dapple the water.
The sun is about to set.
The wind dies down. The ripples
Run red in the sunset.
Suddenly all around us
Are the boats of fishermen
Crying to us to buy their fish.

WANG SHI CH'ENG (WANG I SHANG)

CVII

SUMMER DAY

Reading in the heat of noon
I grow sleepy, put my head
On my arms and fall asleep.
I forget to close the window
And the warm air blows in
And covers my body with petals.

YUAN MEI

CVIII

WINTER NIGHT

It is late in the Winter night.
I am absorbed in a book
And forget to go to bed.
My wife takes my lamp and says,
"Do you know what time it is?"

YUAN MEI

CIX

EVENING LIGHTS ON THE RIVER

Village lights in the dusk,
The fires of the households,
The lamps of the fishing boats,
Sparkle like a swarm of fireflies.

CHIANG SHE CH'UAN

CX

TWILIGHT IN THE RIVER PAVILION

I lean on my rustic gate
Above the swift river
In the evening and hear
The distant sound of women
Beating clothes. The little bridge
Arches over the fishes
And turtles. Once in a great while
Someone crosses. A reflection
Appears on the water, then is gone.

CHIANG SHE CH'UAN

CXI

ON HIS THIRTY-THIRD BIRTHDAY

More than thirty years have rushed
By me like a runaway
Chariot. I too have spent
My life rushing here and there
From one end of the country
To the other. I long for
The homestead where I was born,
A thousand mountain ranges
Away. Like yellow leaves in
The decline of Summer a
Few white hairs have already
Appeared on my head. All my
Travels only made tracks
In drifting sand. I piled up
Learning like a snowball.
I crossed mountains and passed
Examinations and gave
Learned speeches. What did I gain?
Better I stayed home
And raised prize melons.

CH'ANG KUO FAN

CXII

IN THE MOUNTAIN VILLAGE

Wild flowers and grass grow on
The ancient ceremonial
Stairs. The sun sets between the
Forested mountains. The swallows
Who nested once in the painted
Eaves of the palaces of
The young prince are flying
This evening between the homes
Of woodcutters and quarrymen.

More ancient by far than the stairs
Are the cyclopean walls
Of immense dry laid stones covered
With moss and ferns. If you approach
Quietly and imitate their
Voices, you can converse all day
With the tree frogs who live there.

WANG HUNG KUNG

ANONYMOUS FOLK SONGS. Beginning with the *Shi Ching, The Book of Odes*, whose editing was attributed to Confucius, it has been the custom in China periodically to make extensive collections of folk song, "to ascertain what the people are thinking." No other culture seems ever to have done this, although it is a most astute idea. Today it is obvious that popular folk and protest songs reflect the profound dissatisfaction with a murderous social system. Although the classical Chinese, following the Confucian commentaries on *The Book of Odes*, interpreted simple erotic lyrics and narrative ballads as allegorical statements of political criticism, this is not as outrageous as it seemed to earlier generations of Western translators. Of course there is nothing of the one-to-one correspondence of erotic metaphor to political fact the Confucianists persuaded themselves existed, but we are well aware that the love songs of a Donovan, Judy Collins, Joni Mitchell, or Leonard Cohen are quite as subversive of the society which produced them as any overt song of protest. The Han poems are usually serious and seem to have been literary reworkings of folk songs in the *yueh fu* meter. However, the Southern Six Dynasties collections are simple, erotic lyrics, probably sung by courtesans. Many are attributed to legendary girls — Tzu Yeh, T'ao Yeh, and the tragic Maid of Hua Mountain. Like the *Shi Ching* love songs, recent scholarship has arranged many of the Tzu Yeh songs in dialogue between a young man and a girl, and seen them as part of a harvest festival marriage or group marriage celebration. The Northern Six Dynasties *yueh fu* are harder, more literary, more masculine, and show the influence of the peoples beyond the northern frontiers.

CHANG CHI (author of "Night at Anchor by Maple Bridge") lived in the eighth century under the Emperor Hsuan Tsung in the great age of the T'ang Dynasty.

CHANG CHI, a poet of the later T'ang Dynasty, and author of "Faithful Wife," lived in the ninth century. (There were two different poets with this name as spelled in English. The Chi's are different in Chinese.)

CHIANG CHIEH lived at the end of the Sung Dynasty, in the last quarter of the thirteenth century. He became a hermit rather than take office under the Yuan (Mongol) Dynasty.

CHIANG SHE CH'UAN lived from 1725 to 1784.

CHU CHEN PO was a ninth-century poet. A wonderful bestiary could be made up by selections from the whole body of classical Chinese poetry (including "Hedgehog") and illustrated with classical Chinese or Japanese paintings. I recommend the idea to some children's book publisher.

THE POETESS CHU SHU CHEN. Information about the Poetess Chu Shu Chen is all guesswork, based on her poems. She almost certainly lived late in the Sung Dynasty, after Su Tung P'o and Ju Shih; doubtful legends connect her with both. These great Chinese women poets, of which Chu Shu Chen and Li Ch'ing Chao are the two most famous of the Sung Dynasty, are sisters of Christine de Pisan, Gaspara Stampa, and Louise Labé. There has been no writer like them in English, although a similar sensibility is found, in a religious form, in Christina Rossetti.

CH'ANG CH'U LING (673-740) was a counselor of the Emperor Hsuan Tsung of the T'ang Dynasty — called Ming Huang, "The Bright Emperor."

CH'ANG KUO FAN lived in the nineteenth century. The stability of the Chinese tradition and way of life is shown by the echo of this poem across the centuries from the nineteenth-century poets to Hsieh Ling Yun (385-433) in the Time of Troubles in the Six Dynasties, and from him back to Ch'u Yuan (322 B. C.) of the Warring Kingdoms.

THE POETESS CH'EN T'AO, not to be confused with the ninth-century hermit poet Ch'en Sung Po (Ch'en T'ao), was the wife of a Sung Dynasty general.

CH'EN YU YI lived from 1090 to 1138.

CH'IEN CH'I lived in the eighth century. "Visit to the Hermit Ts'ui" is a bread and butter note; the finest such poem is probably the Japanese *waka* echoing Wang Wei:

> Although it was not my own home
> The wild plum by the window
> Smelled just the same.

THE EMPEROR CH'IEN WEN OF LIANG (503-551). An exceptionally large number of the emperors of the Six Dynasties and Three Kingdoms were poets, probably due, as in Japan's Time of Troubles, to the fact that the emperors of the contending states were mostly *rois fainéants*. Power was in the hands of warlords of the type the Japanese stabilized in the Shogunate.

CH'IN CH'ANG SIU. "Spring Sorrow" is a T'ang Dynasty poem, possibly a folk song. She is dreaming of her husband.

CH'U CH'UANG I (early eighth century) was a close friend of the first major T'ang poet and landscapist Wang Wei.

FAN YUN (451-505) was a courtier of the Emperor Wu of Liang. This poem is answered by that of his friend Shen Yueh.

FU HSUAN (217-278) wrote this poem as a literary imitation of the folk songs of the Six Dynasties, the southern style *yueh fu*.

HAN YU (768-824) was the most famous of the prose writers of the T'ang Dynasty and one of the first thinkers to whom the term Neo-Confucian can be strictly applied. This is his most famous poem. On the whole Han Yu seems a rather formal writer, devoid of original ideas.

HO CH'E CH'ANG (659-744) was an official under the Bright Emperor and a drinking companion of LI PO.

HO HSUN (d. 527) was a contemporary and friend of LIU HSIAO CH'AO, SHEN YUEH and FAN YUN.

HSIEH LING YUEN (385-433), Duke of K'ang Lo, was one of the most important poets of the Six Dynasties period. He grew up in the Chin Kingdom where his great grand-uncle Hsieh An had been prime minister and his grandfather a field marshal. At the fall of the Chin Dynasty he became an important official of the Liu Sung. Although his reputation is based upon his nature poetry, meditative elegiac verse describing mountain hermitages, monasteries, or lonely travel, of a type that would have a great influence on Tu Fu, he was actually the proprietor of an immense estate where his fantastic landscaping—at the expense of hundreds of forced laborers—made him enemies in all the surrounding country. He seems to have been restless there, unable to let politics alone, however much he objected to it. Eventually he was demoted from high office and sent to Canton where again he made enemies and finally was executed. He was apparently a rather manic individual and never at rest even at his elaborate retreat. He should have a minor place as a culture hero—he invented mountaineering boots. His poetry is remarkable for its dramatic sonority, rather as if Wordsworth had been rewritten by Marlowe. In his youth Neo-Taoism, and in his maturity Buddhism of a kind related to Zen (Ch'an in Chinese, Dhyana in Sanskrit), the School of Instant Enlightenment, played an explicit role in his poetry. He himself not only wrote poems and essays on the Doctrine of Instant Enlightenment, but read Sanskrit and translated several sutras, accomplishments unheard of among important Chinese poets. I find his poetry rather stiff, not unlike that of Ch'u Yuan, the ancestor of all the unhappy courtier poets. Although Hsieh Ling Yuen's verse for his day was extremely modern, even modernistic, there is also something archaizing about it.

Hsieh Ngao lived at the end of the thirteenth century, during the final days of the Southern Sung. When the Mongols sacked Hangchow he fled to the mountains and spent the rest of his life as a wandering hermit.

Hsin Ch'i Chi (1140-1207) was a general, courtier, and friend of Su Tung P'o and the philosopher Chu Shi. On the fall of the Northern Sung to the Mongols he fled to Hangchow to the Emperor Kao Tsung where he became a general, the governor of provinces and the leader of expeditions attempting the reconquest of the North.

Huang T'ing Ch'ien (1045-1105) was a friend of Su Tung P'o. "Clear Bright" is the Spring Feast of the Dead.

Kao Chi (1336-1374) was the most popular poet of the early Ming Dynasty. He was eventually executed. He led the revival of the classic style of the great T'ang poets.

Kuan Yun She lived in the thirteenth century. Seven-Seven, according to myth is the time when for one night the cowboy, Altair, crosses the Milky Way on a bridge of magpies to sleep with Vega, the weaving girl.

THE POETESS LI CHI'NG CHAO (1084-1142) belongs in the great
company of Gaspara Stampa and Louise Labé. Although the
poems sound like conventional "abandoned love" verses because
they take off from the standard set piece, "The Deserted Concu-
bine" (as in Li Po's "The Jeweled Stairs Grievance," translated by
Pound), they are actually truly personal, written after the death of
her husband. Her father was a friend of Su Tung P'o. She is China's
greatest poetess, of any period. *Wu t'ung* trees — *Sterculia plantani-
folia* — look like planes or sycamores. Nine-Nine — a day of picnics
on hills, chrysanthemum viewing, and outdoor love-making —
was originally both a harvest festival and the Autumn Feast of
the Dead. "Orchid Boat" — her sex, or specifically her vulva.

LI P'IN wrote in the latter half of the ninth century. One of the
most perfect poems of the later T'ang, "Crossing Han River"
sums up the troubled times of the dying dynasty.

LI SHANG YIN lived from 813 to 859. If Tu Fu is to be compared
to Baudelaire, Li Shang Yin in his more complex poems might
be compared with Mallarmé. Yet underlying their complexities
are extremely simple poetic situations of the most classic Chinese
type. Although their poetry was comparatively unappreciated in
the West until recently, a deeper knowledge of T'ang Dynasty
poetic language and greater sophistication of poetic taste have led
to contemporary revaluation. Today Li Shang Yin is considered
the greatest T'ang poet after Po Chu I.

LIU CH'ANG CH'ING lived in the eighth century.

LIU YU HSI lived from 772 to 842.

LU CHI (261-303). Author of a famous *Ars Poetica*, one of the
first and best in the Orient. Lu Chi was a military adventurer and
courtier who was executed in the Six Dynasty struggles for the
throne of Chin.

LU KUEI MENG lived in the ninth century.

LU YU (1125-1209) is the least classical of the major Sung poets.
Although a member of the scholar gentry, he never attained, or
desired, high office, and seems to have been genuinely far from
rich, especially toward the end of his life. (Understand that
throughout China's history a really "poor farmer" never got a

chance to read or write anything.) His poetry is loose, casual. It had to be—he wrote about eleven thousand poems. His best poems have that easy directness that is supposed to come only with rare, concentrated effort. By his day Sung China had retreated to the South and the Golden Tatars in the North were already being threatened by the Mongols who were soon to overwhelm all. Lu Yu's patriotism was not prepared to accept the *modus vivendi* less doctrinaire minds had worked out, and his stirring agitational poems against the invader have been very popular in twentieth-century China where everybody has been an invader to everybody else.

MENG HAO JAN (689-740) was a friend of Wang Wei and one of the leading poets of the early years of the T'ang Dynasty. His middle years were spent as a hermit in the mountains. He is famous for having hidden under Wang Wei's bed when the Emperor Hsuan Tsung came to call. Having offended the Emperor, he was not given a post and went happily back to his hermitage.

NG SHAO lived in the sixth century.

LADY P'AN was a favorite concubine of the Emperor Ch'eng Ti of Han (32 B. C.). Discarded by him, she wrote one of the first and best "deserted courtesan" poems, which would be imitated innumerable times in the centuries to come.

P'AN YUEH (P'AN YENG JEN), of the fourth century, was considered the most handsome man of his time. He became an important official, but like so many others in the Six Dynasties, was eventually executed. Although women are said to have rioted in the streets whenever he went by, he is most famous for his poems to his dead wife.

PAO YU was a monk of the fifth century.

PO CHU I (772-846) is generally considered, with Li Po, Wang Wei, and Tu Fu, one of the four leading poets of the T'ang Dynasty. More varied in his subjects than the others, he was a master of poignant, unforgettable phrases, many of which could be excerpted and stand alone as separate poems. It is this latter characteristic as much as anything else which accounts for his tremendous popularity with the classical poets of Japan, where, as Arthur Waley points out, he is revered as a god of poetry. He was a great favorite of Waley's, whose translations of Po Chu I are among the finest poems of the twentieth century, and who also wrote an excellent biography of Po which everyone interested in Chinese verse, culture, or history should read. It is unequaled as an introduction to the life of the T'ang Dynasty.

SHEN YUEH (441-513) was one of the circle of poets at the court of the Emperor Wu of Liang which included Fan Yun. Shen is extremely important in the evolution of Chinese verse. He popularized a factor in Chinese verse peculiar to the language, the conscious prosodic arrangement of the tones. He was also a severe critic of over-elaboration and references to the classics, older poems, and bits of legend and history. However, this poem refers to a story in the Han Fei book of how Chang Min sought his friend Kao Hui in a dream but got lost in the dream and had difficulty finding his way back.

SU TUNG P'O (1036-1101), named Su Shih, belonged to a powerful family of officials and scholars. Under the protection of his father's patron, Ou Yang Hsiu, he rose to prominence when very young. At first he held various provincial posts. Shortly after he was called to office he came into conflict with the famous reformer, Wang An Shih. I should explain that the early years of Sung witnessed a tremendous increase in trade and rise in the general standard of living. Wang proposed to stem this rising tide of commercialism with a series of economic measures which returned all power to the central authority and curbed, in fact attempted to abolish, the mercantile classes and reform the agricultural system. It has been called, with little accuracy, a program of state socialism and autarchy. Actually it was the purest "Neo-Confucianism" of a kind different from that which, as a philosophy, later acquired the name. But the scholar gentry — the Confucianists — were violently opposed. Wang An Shih was simply too unconventional for them. However, for a time, under a new emperor, his schemes were put into effect, with doubtful results. As one of Wang's leading opponents Su Tung P'o then entered upon a period of remarkable vicissitudes. He first was moved out of the court to the governorship of Hangchow and then was exiled altogether, once as far away as Hainan. His life was a series of ups and downs — out to exile, back to court, out to exile again. He even spent three months in prison. He seems to have been a good, conventional administrator, loved by the people under him but arrogant and rash with equals or supervisors. He was also an excellent painter; his ink paintings of bamboos are superlative. They are imitated to this day and crude forgeries can be found in curio shops. As a painter and something of an esthetician he was one of the founders of the Southern Sung style, one of the glories of Far Eastern culture. He is certainly one of the ten greatest Chinese poets. His work may be full of quotations and allusions to T'ang poetry, T'ao Ch'ien and the classics, but it is still intensely personal and is the climax of early Sung subjectivity. His world is not Tu Fu's: where the latter sees definite particulars, clear moral issues, and bright sharp images, Su Tung P'o's vision is clouded with the all-dissolving systematic doubt of Buddhism and the nihilism of revived philosophical Taoism. Su's is a less precise world, but a vaster one, more like our own.

Su Wu (second century) was a general of the Emperor Wu Ti of Han.

Tu Fu (713-770) is translated at length in my *One Hundred Poems from the Chinese*. Tu Fu is, in my opinion, and in the opinion of a majority of those qualified to speak, the greatest non-epic, non-dramatic poet who has survived in any language. Sappho, for instance, can hardly be said to have survived. He shares with her, Catullus, and Baudelaire, his only possible competitors, a sensibility acute past belief. Like them, he is — possibly paying the price of such a sensibility — considerably neurasthenic and the creator of an elaborate poetic personality, a fictional character half mask, half revelation. Tu Fu came from a family of scholars, officials, and landowners, and rose early to a minor office in the court of Hsuan Tsung, called Ming Huang, the Bright Emperor. With the majority of the scholar class, he was violently opposed to the party of Yang Kuei Fei, the Emperor's famous concubine. Following the legendary histories of the first dynasties, the disasters that smote the Chinese throne were traditionally attributed to the evils of women, eunuchs, wine, and magic, and Ming Huang was no exception.

Actually, Yang Kuei Fei, her family and lovers were the inner core of an imperialist party in the Chinese court. Outlanders and upstarts of various sorts, themselves products of a kind of internationalism, they realized that T'ang China could survive at its then great extent only by admitting the associated peoples of the inner Asian frontiers to a share of power and a measure of federated autonomy. This of course was rank atheist nihilism to the Confucian literati. The court struggle led eventually to the overthrow of Yang Kuo Chung, Yang Kuei Fei's brother; the revolt of An Lu Shan, her Turkish lover; the flight of the court; the execution, during the flight, at the insistence of the orthodox party, of Yang Kuei Fei; the abdication of the Emperor; the recapture of the capital by the troops of his son; and finally the fall of the capital again to the Nan Chao federation of Yunnanese and Tibetans. For a generation the most stable area in China was the isolated Southwest province of Szechuan—a situation not unlike the recent period of Japanese invasion and civil wars. The T'ang Dynasty was crippled permanently. The greatest period of Chinese civilization in the Christian era entered a slow decline from which it never recovered and the seeds were sown of a parochial chauvinism which kept the so-called geo-political problems of China unsolved until now.

Although Tu Fu's young days were spent at Ming Huang's spectacularly brilliant court, familiar to most Western readers from the work of Li Po, his maturity was passed in a time of trouble, wandering, exile, and chronic insecurity. He became a Court Censor, a kind of Tribune of the Patricians, under Su Tsung, Ming Huang's son. This job was in reality an empty sinecure. Tu Fu, an unregenerate believer in the classics, proceeded to admonish the Emperor on his morals and foreign policy and was summarily dismissed. The longest settled period in his life followed, in a "thatched hut" in the suburbs of Ch'eng-tu in Szechuan. It may have had a grass roof but it was doubtless quite palatial by any standards other than those of the imperial palace. He was happy, as men usually are, in quiet revery over vanished glories and a ruined career. Political changes started him wandering again slowly down the river, always hoping to return to the capital. His last years were spent largely in a houseboat. At 57 he died, apparently still in his boat. Various legends grew up about his death. Possibly he died of exposure due to the vicissitudes of storm and flood on the river.

All through his life Tu Fu wrote full-dress poems of advice to the throne. Most of these are the expected thing, as full of wisdom as a Papal Christmas message, but in time he seems to have learned. Almost alone of his class, at the end of his days, he came to hope for a united Chinese commonwealth, under a somewhat less pretentious, or, like the British, more etherealized, cult of the throne. I have not translated any of these poems. Others have done them well. They would require too much explanation. However well intentioned, they savor of the social lie, at least to my taste, and do not interest me. I have chosen only those poems whose appeal is simple and direct, with a minimum of allusion to past literature or contemporary politics—in other words, poems that speak to me of situations in life like my own. I have thought of my translations as, finally, expressions of myself.

I do not wish to give the impression that Tu Fu is faultless. He was a member of the scholar gentry and suffered from their ethnocentrism and caste consciousness, however transfigured. He was a valetudinarian. By the time he was thirty he was referring to himself as an aged white-haired man. He constantly speaks of his home as a hut and complains of his poverty, while in other poems, written at the same time, he reveals that he was moderately rich. He seems never to have relinquished ownership of his various farms ("grass huts") and probably always drew revenue or at least credit from them. It is greatly to be doubted if either he or any of his family ever suffered from hunger, let alone starvation. True, he says his son starved to death, but this may be only a literary expression. With the collapse of central authority and the resultant famine, many people died of starvation. His son died at the same time, more likely from pestilence. He seems to have had only a mild literary affection for his wife. He wrote no love poems to women. Like most of his caste then and now his passionate relationships were with men. But these are not even minor faults—they are conventions, literary, caste, or Chinese. They are certainly microscopic spots compared with the blemishes that envelop Baudelaire like blankets. In Tu Fu, behind the conventions is a humanity as deep and wise as Homer's.

Tu Fu comes from a saner, older, more secular culture than Homer and it is not a new discovery with him that the gods, the abstractions and forces of nature, are frivolous, lewd, vicious, quarrelsome, and cruel, and only men's stead-fastness, love, magnanimity, calm, and compassion redeem the nightbound world. It is not a discovery, culturally or historically, but it is the essence of his being as a poet. If Isaiah is the greatest religious poet, Tu Fu is not religious at all. But for me his response to the human situation is the only kind of religion likely to outlast this century. "Reverence for life," it has been called. I have saturated myself with his poetry for forty-five years. I am sure he has made me a better man, as a moral agent and as a perceiving organism. I say this because I feel that, above a certain level of attainment, the greatest poetry answers out of hand the problems of the critic and the esthetician. Poetry like Tu Fu's is the answer to the question, "What is the purpose of Art?"

Tu Mu (803-852) was, with Po Chu I and Li Shang Yin, one of the leading poets of the latter part of the T'ang Dynasty. His poems blend the influences of Tu Fu, T'ao Yuan Ming and Wang Wei into an amalgam considerably softer than their originals. The second poem is capable of a sexual interpretation.

T'ao Hung Ching (T'ao T'ung Ming) (452-536) began his career as a tutor to the Emperor's children but soon resigned and spent his life as a Taoist hermit devoted to alchemy, yogic exercises and deep contemplation. He was universally venerated and consulted by statesmen and visited by the Emperor Wu of Liang himself. Verses such as these erotic poems by monks and hermits (especially the Neo-Taoist ones) are susceptible of a mystical interpretation, like the poems of Hafiz or St. Mechtild. Conversely, to this day there are Chinese, scholars, not cranks, who interpret the *Li Sao*, the *Tao Te Ching* and the famous "mystical" passage of Mencius in what we would call a tantric sense. The pivotal passage in all Chinese literature is the sixth chapter, the most cryptic, of the *Tao Te Ching*:

> The valley's soul is deathless.
> It is called the Dark Woman.
> The Dark Woman is the gate
> To the root of heaven and earth.
> If you draw her out like floss
> She is inexhaustible.
> She is only to be possessed without effort.

T'ao Yuan Ming (Tao Chin) (365-427) was the greatest poet of the Six Dynasties. As Hsieh Lung Yuen is called the inventor of mountain and waterfall poetry, so T'ao Yuan Ming is called the father of fields and gardens poetry. He spent eighty days in a minor government post, then fled to the country and never returned. His poems established a style and a poetic situation which was to last until the Communist regime. Wang Wei and Lu Yu are only two out of thousands of his descendants. His poetry is quiet and unpretentious, limpid in sound and forthright in meaning. He is one of the very greatest Chinese poets of all time. He has been translated several times, notably by Arthur Waley.

T'ien Hung was one of the warlords in the struggles out of which the Han Dynasty came in the third century B. C. This poem is a *yueh fu*, an imitation folk song, and is of disputed authorship.

Ts'ui Hao (eighth century) was a friend of Li Po.

Wang Chang Ling died about 756 in the revolt of An Lu Shan against the T'ang Emperor Hsuan Tsung.

Wang Hung Kung is a contemporary poet.

Wang Shi Ch'eng (Wang I Shang) (1634-1711) was a typical intellectual functionary of the Ming Dynasty; his poetry refined the forms of the past and considerably reduced their profundity. There was another poet of the same name, Wang Yuan Mei, 1526-1590, who wrote "A Note of Thanks":

> I thank you for your gift
> Of a thousand silver pieces
> But I beg you to take them back.
> All the riches in the world
> Will soon wear out, but my heart
> Is more lasting and without price.

Wang Wei (701-761) was with Li Po and Tu Fu one of the great poets of the reign of the Emperor Hsuan Tsung. He was captured by An Lu Shan and after the rebellion was imprisoned for a short time. The rest of his life was spent in retreat in the mountains. Also a great painter, he is usually credited with the invention of the contemplative landscape which was to reach its greatest development in the Sung Dynasty and in Japan. Like Su Tung

P'o he is considered one of the very greatest calligraphers of all time; his style is still carefully imitated. The only poet whose poems of hermitage, out of all the hundreds of thousands written in China, can be compared with his is T'ao Yuan Ming. Wang was also considered the leading musician of his time. He was given the cabinet office of Minister of Music, a position far more important in Chinese civilization than it would seem to us. His poems have a compactness and ordonnance which makes them seem much more architectural or classical than many others on the same subject. In this they resemble his paintings, which survive in copies, and which are as tightly organized as a Cubist's. His poems are inexhaustible expressions of the Doctrines of Mind Only and The Void; yet they are as unpretentious (if not as casual) as those of Lu Yu who wrote 11,000 poems. Wang Wei is one of those model poets, personally and artistically flawless, who occur very rarely in the history of literature.

WEN T'ING YEN (ninth century) was a friend of Li Shang Yin.

THE EMPEROR WU OF HAN (156-187), whose name was Liu Ch'u, was a patron of literature and the arts who traveled extensively about his kingdom and deeply mourned the loss of a favorite wife. For these reasons a number of poems on such subjects, some of them of great beauty, have been attributed to him, but the only one accepted by all modern scholars as being his was written on the rupture of a great dike and in the style of Chu Yuan's *Li Sao*. The poems of sorrow for lost love are far more accessible to modern taste — or to nearly any taste. They were to have a great influence on future Chinese verse and were specifically imitated by the Sung Dynasty poet Mei Yao Ch'en whose poems are given in my *One Hundred Poems From the Chinese*.

THE EMPEROR WU OF LIANG (464-549) was also named Hsiao Tsu Yun. The Hsiao royal family was very productive of poets, probably because they had become, like the Japanese emperors, purely ceremonial rulers confined to ritual appearances and to their harems. The Hsiaos founded a school of erotic verse, known appropriately in Chinese as "harem poetry," which would endure until the end of the Manchu Dynasty in the twentieth century. Such poetry may have been written in the palace, but its connections with the folk songs of professional courtesans and prostitutes, from which it derived and to which it returned as an influence, give it a languid, poignant reality very like those Japanese *waka* by emperors or Fujiwara princes which are still sung in a folk-song meter (*dodoitsu*) by geisha to this day.

Hsiao Tsu Yun was the founder of the dynasty. His brother Hsiao Tzu Hui, Hsiao Kang (the Emperor Chien Wen), and his brother Hsiao T'ung were all poets. Like almost everybody of importance in the Six Dynasties period, most of them came to an unfortunate end. The number of people who were murdered, were executed or committed suicide in China in the fifth and sixth centuries is hair-raising. It is hard to understand how the society functioned at all. Surprisingly, unlike the European Dark Ages, it was a period of great accomplishment in literature, learning and the arts, and cultural patterns were established then which came to flower and fruit in the T'ang and Sung Dynasties.

WU WEI YE (1609-1671) was a courtier of the last Ming Emperor. At the fall of the dynasty he went into retirement for ten years, but in his old age he was persuaded to return to the Manchu court. Although the poem "At Yuen Yang Lake" may well record an actual occurrence, and is also indebted to poems by Tu Fu and Su Tung P'o and Lu Yu, it is an excellent example of the possibilities for political interpretation usually missed by Western readers.

THE EMPEROR YANG OF SUI. The brief Sui Dynasty (581-617) suppressed the contending powers of the Six Dynasties and handed on a unified Chinese Empire to the T'ang. It was a period of the rapid spread of Buddhism and developed characteristically Chinese Buddha and Bodhisattva images.

YUAN CHI (210-263) was one of the famous Seven Sages of the Bamboo Grove and as such one of the founders of literary-philosophical Neo-Taoism. This poem is one of eighty.

YUAN MEI (1716-1797) was one of the most intimate and natural of the poets of the Ch'ing or Manchu Dynasty, a time generally of considerable preciosity.

134

SELECT BIBLIOGRAPHY

(Arranged chronologically by publication dates)

The Chinese Classics, James Legge, London, 1870.

Lyrics from the Chinese, Helen Waddell, London & Boston. From the Jesuits' excellent Latin.

Cathay, Ezra Pound, London, 1915. Few, perfect, a classic in English, Pound's best verse.

170 Chinese Poems, Arthur Waley, London & New York, 1918. Excellent.

Chinese Lyrics from the Book of Jade, French of Judith Gautier, translated by James Whitall, New York, 1918. Misses the lassitude of her French.

Coloured Stars, E. Powys Mathers, London & Boston, 1918. Highly colored, from the French.

More Translations from the Chinese, Arthur Waley, London & New York, 1918. Excellent.

The Garden of Bright Waters, E. Powys Mathers, London & Boston, 1920. Both Mathers' are reissued by Knopf.

Fir Flower Tablets, Amy Lowell & Florence Ayscough, Boston, 1920. Very good.

The Works of Li Po, Shigeyoshi Obata, London & New York, 1922. Good.

The Temple and Other Poems, Arthur Waley, London & New York, 1923. Excellent.

The Lost Flute, French of Franz Toussaint, translated by G. L. Joerissen, London, 1923. Fair.

Lotus and Chrysanthemum, anthology, J. L. French, New York, 1927. None too good.

Tu Fu, Florence Ayscough, London & Boston, 1929. Excellent.

The Jade Mountain (300 Poems of T'ang), Witter Bynner, New York, 1929. Excellent, Bynner's best verse.

Images in Jade, Arthur Christy, New York, 1929. Fair.

Selections from Su Tung P'o, C. D. Le G. Clark, London, 1931. Very good.

Festivals and Songs of Ancient China, Marcel Granet, London & New York, 1932. Essential.

Poetry of the Orient, Eunice Tietjens, New York, 1934. Fair.

The Way and Its Power (Tao Te Ching), Arthur Waley, London & New York, 1934. Excellent.

Travels of a Chinese Poet (Tu Fu, Volume II), F. Ayscough, London & New York, 1934. Excellent.

The Prose Poetry of Su Tung P'o, C. D. Le G. Clark, Shanghai, 1935. Excellent.

Modern Chinese Poetry, Acton and Ch'en, London, 1936. Very good.

The Book of Songs, Arthur Waley, London & New York, 1937. Excellent.

Chinese Lyrics, Chu Ta-kao, Cambridge, 1937. Fair.

The White Pony, anthology, edited by Robert Payne, New York, 1947. Very good.

Contemporary Chinese Poetry, edited by Robert Payne, New York, 1947. Very good.

The Gay Genius (Su Tung P'o), Lin Yu Tang, New York, 1947. Biased.

Po Chu-i, Arthur Waley, London & New York, 1949. Very good.

The Book of Odes, Bernhard Karlgren, Stockholm, 1950. The best Shi Ching.

Li Po, Arthur Waley, London & New York, 1950. Only "good," he doesn't like Li Po.

The Art of Letters, E. R. Hughes, New York, 1951. Very illuminating, too much influence of I. A. Richards.

Tao the Hermit, William Acker, New York & London, 1952. Good.

Tu Fu, William Hung, Cambridge, Mass., 1952. Very good, if a little prosaic.

Poems of T'ao Ch'ien, Chang and Sinclair, Honolulu, 1953. Good.

The Confucian Odes (Shi Ching), Ezra Pound, Cambridge, Mass., 1954. The less said the better.

The Nine Songs, Arthur Waley, London, 1955. Very good.

Poems of Lee Hou-chu (Li Yu), Liu Yih-ling and Shahid Suhrawardy, Bombay, 1948.

Leaves from Chinese History in Verse, Li Chin-lun, New York, 1952. A general anthology.

Lin Ho-ching (Lin Pu), Max Perleberg, Hong Kong, 1952.

The Book of Songs (Shi Ching), Arthur Waley, London & New York, 1954. Definitive.

One Hundred Poems from the Chinese, Kenneth Rexroth, New York, 1956. Thirty-five poems of Tu Fu, the rest Sung.

Yuan Mei, Arthur Waley, London & New York, 1956. Poems and biography. Excellent translations and picture of eighteenth-century China.

Why I Live on the Mountain, C. H. Kwôck and Vincent McHugh, San Francisco, 1958.

The Jade Necklace, Lin San Kwei, verse rendered by Stanwood Cobb, Washington, 1958. A T'ang anthology.

Ch'u Tz'ŭ, The Songs of the South, David Hawkes, Oxford & New York, 1959. Very good.

Chinese Love Poems, D. Klemer, illustrated by Seong Moy, Garden City, 1959. Gift book.

The Literary Mind and the Carving of Dragons, Liu Hsieh, translated by V. Yu-chung Shih, New York, 1959. A major work of Six Dynasties literary criticism and poetics. Excellent introduction and notes.

Poems of Solitude, Jerome Ch'en and Michael Bullock, London & New York, 1960. A general anthology.

The Jade Flute, Mount Vernon, New York, 1960. A gift book.

The Penguin Book of Chinese Verse, edited by Albert Richard Davis, translated by Robert Kotewall and Norman L. Smith, Harmondsworth, Middlesex & Baltimore, 1962.

Cold Mountain (Han Shan), Burton Watson, New York, 1962. Good. Snyder's version is better.

The Poet Kao Ch'i, F. W. Mote, Princeton, 1962. A biography with poems, excellent as a picture of the troubled times of transition from the Mongol Dynasty to the Ming. Translations good.

The Art of Chinese Poetry (Liu Lo-yu), James J. Y. Liu, London & Chicago, 1962. Good.

Lament Everlasting (The Death of Yang Kuei-fei) (Po Chu-I), Howard S. Levy, Tokyo, 1962.

The Moment of Wonder, edited by Richard Lewis, illustrated, New York, 1964. Chinese and Japanese poetry.

Poems of the Late T'ang, A. C. Graham, Baltimore, 1965. Good.

Cold Mountain Poems (Han Shan), Gary Snyder, San Francisco, 1965. Excellent.

A Collection of Chinese Lyrics, Duncan Robert Mackintosh, London & Nashville, 1965. Poor.

Su Tung P'o (Su Shih), Burton Watson, New York, 1965. Good.
The Murmuring Stream (Hsieh Ling Yun), J. D. Frodsham, O.U.P.,
Kuala Lumpur & New York, 1967. Excellent biography and
poems; translations accurate but prosaic.
An Anthology of Chinese Verse, J. D. Frodsham and Ch'eng Hsi,
O.U.P., Oxford & New York, 1967. Excellent. Includes verse
from the Six Dynasties; first volume of a projected series to
cover all dynasties.
Chinese Moonlight, Walasse Ting, New York, 1967.
A Primer of Tu Fu, David Hawkes, Oxford & New York, 1967.
Gives transliteration in modern orthography of thirty-five
poems, exegesis, literal and prose translations. A bit prosaic, but
invaluable and very sound.
Fifty Songs from the Yüan, Richard Fu-sen Yang and Charles
R. Metzger, London, 1967.
An Introduction to Sung Poetry (Yoshikawa Kōjirō), Burton Wat-
son, Cambridge, Mass., 1967. Good; very square, modern
Japanese taste.
The Poetry of Li Shang-yin, James J. Y. Liu, Chicago, 1969. Poems,
biography, and elaborate exegesis. Excellent.
Cantonese Love Songs, Clementi, Oxford, no date. Very good;
as a volume of texts, unique.
Flower Shadows, Lee, New York, no date. Fair.

Poésies Chinoises de l'Epoque Thang, Hervey St. Denys, Paris,
1862. Still good.
Le Li Sao, Hervey St. Denys, Paris, 1870. Untranslatable, still
the best.
La Poésie Chinoise, C. Imbault-Huart, Paris, 1886. Good.
Un Poète Chinois du XVIII Siècle, C. Imbault-Huart, Shanghai,
1886. Good.
Poésie Moderne, C. Imbault-Huart, Paris, 1892. Good.
Livre de Jade, Judith Gautier, Paris, 1908. Excellent, a French, or
world, classic. The best English translations of Judith Gautier
are the few by the French-American poet Stuart Merrill in his
Pastels and Prose, published about sixty years ago by Harper.
La Flute de Jade, Franz Toussaint, Paris, 1920. Fair.
Fêtes et Chansons Anciennes de la Chine, M. Granet, Paris, 1929.
Essential.

Anthologie de la Littérature Chinoise, Sung-nien Hsu, Paris, 1933. Fair.
T'ao Yuan Ming, Wong Wen Po, Paris, 1934. Good.
Wang Wei, Liou Kin Ling, Paris, 1941. Good.
Cent Quatrains des T'ang, Lo Ta Kang, Paris, 1947. Very good—a lovely book.
Homme d'Abord, Poète Ensuite, Lo Ta Kang, Paris, 1948. Ditto.
Anthologie Raisonnée de la Littérature Chinoise, G. Margouliés, Paris, no date, recent. Excellent.
Florilège des Poèmes Song, Soulié de Morant, Paris, no date. Excellent, second only to J. Gautier.
Die Lieder des Li Yü, Alfred Hoffmann, Köln, 1950.
Poetische Werke (Han Yu), Erwin von Zach, edited with an introduction by James Robert Hightower, Cambridge, U.S.A., 1952.
Gedichte (Tu Fu), Erwin von Zach, edited with an introduction by James Robert Hightower, Cambridge, Mass., 1952.
Nuits de Chine, Yeou Ta, introduction and adaptation by Joséphine, Paris, 1954.
Liriche Cinesi, edited by G. Valensin, Rome, 1954.
La Poésie Chinoise, Patricia Guillermaz, Paris, 1957. Excellent.
Leben und Dichtungen des Ni Tsan, Helga Kuntze-Shroff, Bombay, 1959.
Poesía China, Maria Teresa León and Rafael Alberti, Buenos Aires, 1960. Good, very free, general anthology. Alberti is a major poet.
Poesie del Fiume Wang, Wang Wei and P'ei Ti, translated by Martin Benedikter, Torino, 1961.
Anthologie de la Poésie Chinoise Classique, Paul Demiéville, Paris, 1962. Excellent general anthology.
La Poésie Chinoise Contemporaine, Patricia Guillermaz, Paris, 1962. Excellent.
La Poésie Chinoise, des Origines à la Révolution, Patricia Guillermaz, Paris, 1966. Excellent.
Aux Origines de la Poésie Classique en Chine, Jean Pierre Diény, Leiden, 1968. Very good. Exegesis, texts, translations, general criticism.

The best German versions are still those of Klabund.
There are many new translations in Russian, Swedish, Dutch,

Finnish (those of Pertti Nieminen are among the best contemporary Finnish poetry), Polish, Czech, Bulgarian, Rumanian, Norwegian, Indonesian, Korean (both North and South), and Vietnamese, those in the socialist countries stimulated by the Chinese Communist regime. Japan has witnessed a tremendous burst of activity in Sinology in the past twenty years; to a lesser extent this is also true of Russia. Japanese translation and criticism are dominated by the conventional taste of the Japanese establishment, but there are large and ever-growing minority opinions and tastes which are anything but conventional. Japanese is rapidly becoming a required language for those who would study classical Chinese literature.

There are a number of general works in English of great value: histories of Chinese literature by Lai Ming, Liu Wu-chi, collections like *Wen-lin*, by the University of Wisconsin, *Studies in Chinese Literature* by the Harvard Yen Ching Institute, Hightower's *Topics in Chinese Literature*, Burton Watson's *Early Chinese Literature*, and an immense number of books on Chinese philosophy, civilization, history, and new translations and commentaries on Confucius, Lao Tse, and Chuang Tsu. Especially to be recommended is one of the greatest scholarly works of all time, Joseph Needham's *Science and Civilization in China*, eventually to be many massive volumes. I have included no works of or on twentieth-century Chinese literature, really a different subject, and none on Communist Chinese literature, a different subject again. Translations into English now being issued in Peking are uniformly extremely poor. The Communist government should hire a new editor for their English language publications.

New Directions Paperbooks

Complete descriptive catalog available free on request from
New Directions, 333 Sixth Avenue, New York 10014.   † Bilingual.